RICHARDSON

Find it!

In the backyard

Published by Richardson Publishing Group Limited.
www.richardsonpublishinggroup.com

10 9 8 7 6 5 4 3 2 1

© Richardson Publishing Group Ltd 2022.

Design by Junior London Ltd, junior.london. Illustration by Jonathan Mortimer.

Find it! In the garden ISBN is 978-1-913602-25-3
Find it! In the backyard ISBN is 978-1-913602-26-0

Printed and bound by Bell & Bain Ltd, 303 Burnfield Road, Thornliebank, Glasgow G46 7UQ.

A catalogue record for this book is available from the British Library.

If you would like to comment on any aspect of this book, please contact us at:

E-mail: puzzles@richardsonpublishinggroup.com

🐦 Follow us on Twitter @puzzlesandgames
📷 instagram.com/richardsonpuzzlesandgames
f facebook.com/richardsonpuzzlesandgames

Contents

Introduction

Find it! books are designed to foster a love of learning and exploring the world through having fun.

Each of our books contain twenty-five things to find in the world around you, along with amazing facts and mind-bending puzzles.

Solutions to the puzzles can be found in the back of the book along with a place to make notes on your finds and a summary chart of the things to find. You can use the summary chart as an index to quickly locate your finds within the book or you can cut it out of the book and use it to find things on your travels!

Once you have found everything, there is a certificate at the very back of the book which you can ask a parent or guardian to complete and award to you!

For every 3 books completed, a parent or guardian can send us a message in order to receive a Find it! Super Spotter badge (T&Cs apply)! Simply fill in the form on our website at: richardsonpuzzlesandgames.com/superspotter

Happy finding!

Introduction

Tick this box when you have found the object. If you have a friend or sibling with you, why don't you set up a game to see who can find the most objects each?

Activity to complete!

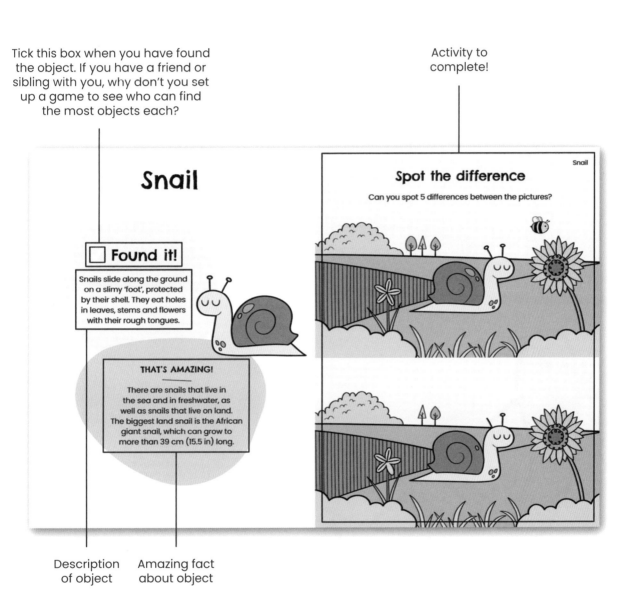

Snail

☐ **Found it!**

Snails slide along the ground on a slimy 'foot', protected by their shell. They eat holes in leaves, stems and flowers with their rough tongues.

THAT'S AMAZING!

There are snails that live in the sea and in freshwater, as well as snails that live on land. The biggest land snail is the African giant snail, which can grow to more than 39 cm (15.5 in) long.

Snail

Spot the difference

Can you spot 5 differences between the pictures?

Description of object

Amazing fact about object

Bird

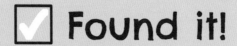 Found it!

Birds are found all over the world, from the cold north and south poles to warm, wet rainforests and dry grasslands. Each type of bird is specially adapted to its home.

THAT'S AMAZING!

Of the thousands of different kinds of bird, there are 60 that can't fly. These include penguins, ostriches, kiwis and emus.

Dot to dot

Connect the dots to uncover a picture, then
fill in with pens or pencils.

Bird feeder

☑ Found it!

Putting out food for birds helps them to survive, especially in cold weather when birds need plenty of energy from food to help keep them warm.

No bird feeder?

Why don't you make one out of an old bottle?

THAT'S AMAZING!

Many birds like to eat seeds, including sunflower seeds, nuts, cooked rice, and fruit. Never leave out salted food, because the salt can be harmful to birds.

Spot the difference

Can you spot 5 differences between the pictures?

Cat

☑ Found it!

Cats are the world's most popular pets, and they have been living happily with people for thousands of years. The Ancient Egyptians thought they were magical animals that could bring good luck to their owners.

THAT'S AMAZING!

Pet cats are cousins of big wild cats. The biggest cat is the Siberian tiger, found in Russia, China and North Korea. It can measure more than 3 m (10 ft) long and weigh 300 kg (660 lb).

Wordsearch

Look for the 10 words hidden in the wordsearch puzzle. The hidden words will run down and across. There are no words that run backwards or on a diagonal.

S	A	V	A	N	N	A	H	H	R
P	B	O	M	B	A	Y	U	I	I
T	G	P	U	C	R	O	O	G	A
S	B	E	N	G	A	L	B	H	C
P	S	R	C	W	R	T	U	L	Y
H	M	S	H	O	P	R	R	A	P
Y	P	I	K	W	F	S	M	N	R
N	G	A	I	B	V	J	E	D	U
X	E	N	N	S	R	R	S	E	S
R	A	G	D	O	L	L	E	R	A

BENGAL   HIGHLANDER   RAGDOLL
BOMBAY   MUNCHKIN   SAVANNAH
BURMESE   PERSIAN   SPHYNX
CYPRUS

Bee

☑ Found it!

There are many different kinds of bee. Bumblebees are the bigger, rounder ones. All bees buzz from flower to flower looking for nectar, which is their food.

THAT'S AMAZING!

As they gather nectar, the dusty pollen inside flowers sticks to bees and other insects. The insects carry the pollen from flower to flower, and this helps make seeds for new plants.

Maze

Guide the bee to the flower.

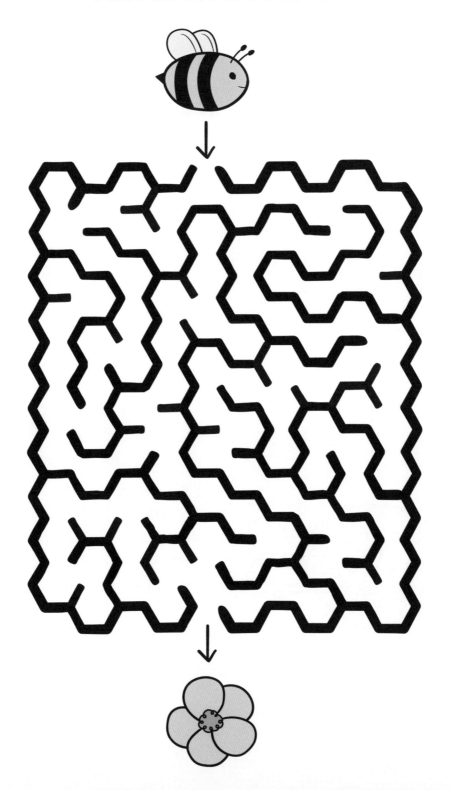

Spider

☑ Found it!

Spiders scuttle along on eight legs. All spiders can make silk, and some make webs to catch smaller insects.

THAT'S AMAZING!
———

Most spiders have eight eyes, as well as eight legs! But some spiders have six eyes, some have four, and there are some spiders that don't have eyes at all.

Spot the difference

Circle the odd one out.

Beetle

☑ Found it!

Like bees and ants, beetles are insects, with three main parts to their body and six legs. Most beetles have two sets of wings – soft ones that they use to fly, and hard ones that close over the soft ones like a protective shield.

THAT'S AMAZING!

Beetles are the most common type of animal on Earth. One in every five living things is a beetle!

Matching pair

Circle the 2 beetles that are the same.

Ant

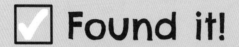 **Found it!**

There are more than 12,000 different kinds of ant in the world. They are insects that live together in big groups called colonies.

THAT'S AMAZING!

Some ants can carry 50 times their own body weight. If you were that strong, you would be able to lift a bison!

Maze

Guide the ant to the ice cream.

Worm

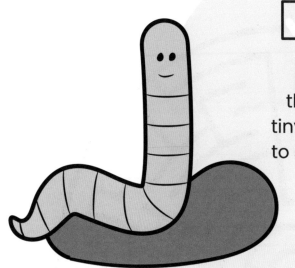

☑ Found it!

Earthworms burrow through the soil eating tiny living things too small to see. They help keep the soil healthy.

THAT'S AMAZING!

The longest animal ever discovered is a worm. A bootlace worm was found measuring 55 m (180 ft), or the length of six buses, and just 2 cm (less than an inch) wide!

Numbers

If you subtract the number of worms in the mud from the number of worms in the grass, how many worms are you left with? Use the number line if you need it.

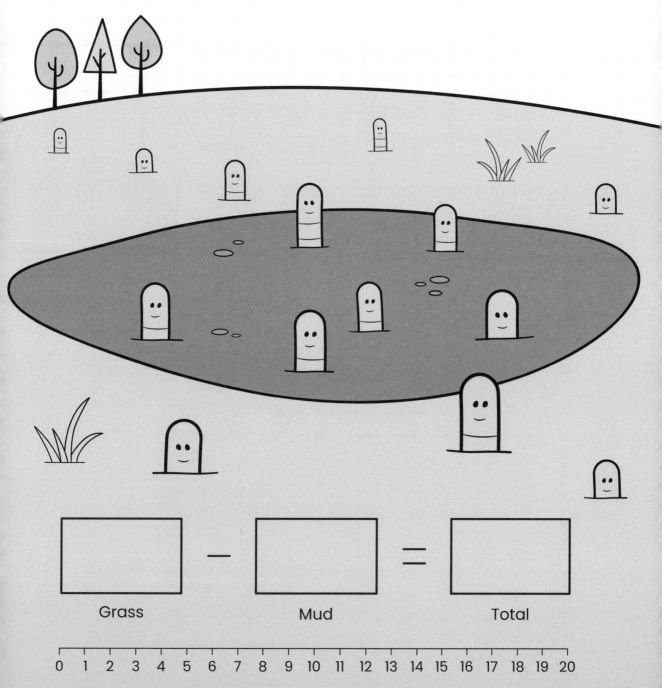

	Grass		Mud		Total

0 1 2 3 4 5 6 7 8 9 10 11 12 13 14 15 16 17 18 19 20

Snail

☑ Found it!

Snails slide along the ground on a slimy 'foot', protected by their shell. They eat holes in leaves, stems and flowers with their rough tongues.

THAT'S AMAZING!

———

There are snails that live in the sea and in freshwater, as well as snails that live on land. The biggest land snail is the African giant snail, which can grow to more than 39 cm (15.5 in) long.

Spot the difference

Can you spot 5 differences between the pictures?

Flower pot

☑ Found it!

All sorts of plants can be grown in pots. You don't need to have a garden to grow flowers, or even vegetables, as long as you have a sunny windowsill.

THAT'S AMAZING!

The most up-to-date flower pots are powered by batteries, and water and feed the plants automatically.

No flower pot?

Why don't you make one out of an empty container?

Complete the picture

Finish the design on the other half of the flower pot.

Vegetable plant

☑ Found it!

If you plant vegetable seeds early in the year, you can be eating tasty vegetables by summer. Underneath these lush green leaves there are carrots waiting to be dug up.

THAT'S AMAZING!

Not all carrots are orange. There are purple, yellow and white ones, but orange carrots became the most popular hundreds of years ago, when they were grown to celebrate the royal House of Orange in Holland.

Complete the words

Complete the names of these different types of vegetable. The images next to the words are a clue. Cover them up if you would like to make the puzzle harder!

P □ □

C □ R R □ T

P □ M P K □ N

C □ B B □ G □

B R □ C C □ L □

P □ T □ T □

Red or pink flower

☑ Found it!

Roses are thorny plants with beautiful flowers that often have a lovely scent.

THAT'S AMAZING!

As well as looking pretty, roses are tasty too. Rose petals can be eaten, and are often used in Middle Eastern cooking. However, don't pick rose petals and eat them – they might have been sprayed to keep away pests and may not be safe to eat.

Draw a picture

What red or pink flowers can you find? Draw them here.

Herb plant

☑ Found it!

Herbs are plants that are used for food, medicine, or for their smell. This is a basil plant— its leaves taste delicious added to pasta sauce or pizza.

THAT'S AMAZING!

Ancient Roman soldiers used to soak the herb thyme in water and use the water to bathe in, because they thought it gave them courage.

Wordsearch

Look for the 10 words hidden in the wordsearch puzzle. The hidden words will run down and across. There are no words that run backwards or on a diagonal.

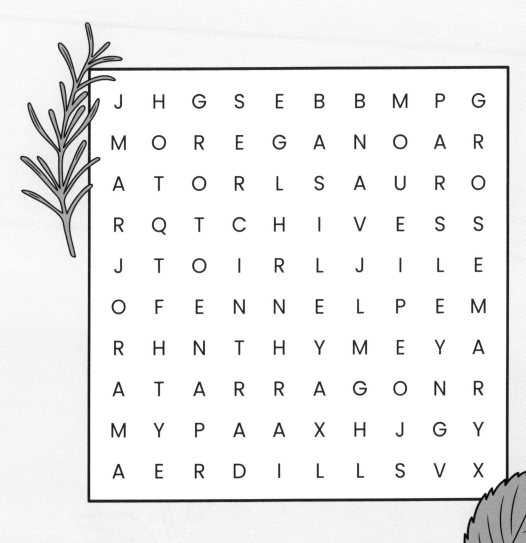

```
J  H  G  S  E  B  B  M  P  G
M  O  R  E  G  A  N  O  A  R
A  T  O  R  L  S  A  U  R  O
R  Q  T  C  H  I  V  E  S  S
J  T  O  I  R  L  J  I  L  E
O  F  E  N  N  E  L  P  E  M
R  H  N  T  H  Y  M  E  Y  A
A  T  A  R  R  A  G  O  N  R
M  Y  P  A  A  X  H  J  G  Y
A  E  R  D  I  L  L  S  V  X
```

BASIL	MARJORAM	ROSEMARY
CHIVE	OREGANO	TARRAGON
DILL	PARSLEY	THYME
FENNEL		

Purple flower

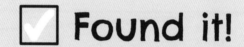

☑ Found it!

These plants with tall purple spires of flowers are called salvias.

THAT'S AMAZING!
———
The herb sage, used in cooking, is also a kind of salvia, even though it looks very different from the ones with purple flowers.

Draw a picture

What purple flowers can you find? Draw them here.

Grass

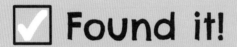 **Found it!**

There are thousands of
different kinds of grass,
from the short grass grown on
lawns; to tall, flowering grasses;
and the wheat and barley used
to make our food.

THAT'S AMAZING!

———

Bamboo is also a type
of grass, and 'Giant
Bamboo' is the tallest
grass in the world.

Maze

Help the lawnmower to find the track to the gate.

Yellow flower

☑ Found it!

Sunflowers are bright
and beautiful. Some kinds
can grow to 3 m (120 in),
and some are even taller.

THAT'S AMAZING!

The tallest ever sunflower was
grown in Germany in 2014.
It measured 9.17 m (30 ft 1 in).

Draw a picture

What yellow flowers can you find? Draw them here.

Weed

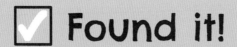 Found it!

Gardeners call plants they don't want in their gardens 'weeds' – they are often very tough, fast-growing plants.

THAT'S AMAZING!

Giant hogweed is one of the biggest weeds in the world. It can grow to over 3 m (10 ft) tall. If a stem is broken, the white sap inside can burn skin.

Spot the difference

Can you spot 5 differences between the pictures?

Soil

☑ Found it!

Soil might look like boring brown stuff, but it's essential for plants. We couldn't live without soil.

THAT'S AMAZING!

Soil is made from sand, clay, silt and water, and rotted down fallen leaves, dead plants and animals, and animal droppings.

Complete the words

Complete the names of the objects that can be composted. The images next to the words are a clue. Cover them up if you would like to make the puzzle harder!

G R ☐ S S

H ☐ R B S

F R ☐ ☐ T

P ☐ P ☐ R

V ☐ G ☐ T ☐ B L ☐ S

F L ☐ W ☐ R S

Fork

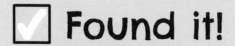 Found it!

A garden fork is a very useful tool for digging. It can be pushed into the earth more easily than a spade, and is less likely to damage plant roots.

THAT'S AMAZING!

The long, thin prongs of a fork are called 'tines'.

Numbers

How many fork handles and how many fork tines are there?

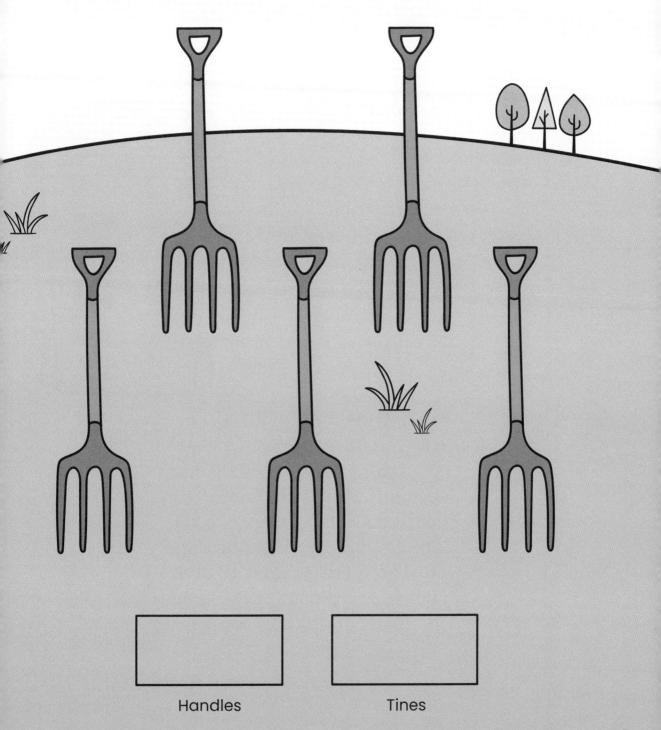

Handles	Tines

Recycling bin

☑ Found it!

We can put lots of things we don't need any more into recycling bins. There are recycling bins for plastic, metal, glass, paper, and cardboard, which can all be used to make new products.

THAT'S AMAZING!

Different materials take different amounts of time to break down, or decompose. Glass doesn't decompose at all. Plastic bags can take 10 to 20 years to break down, and plastic bottles can take hundreds of years.

Maze

Help the truck to find the road to the recycling depot.

Watering can

☑ **Found it!**

Plants need sunshine and water to survive. When it doesn't rain, you might need to water outdoor plants with a watering can.

THAT'S AMAZING!

Watering cans with a handle and a spout were invented around 300 years ago. Before that people used various types of pot, or animal skins filled with water.

Dot to dot

Connect the dots to uncover a picture, then
fill in with pens or pencils.

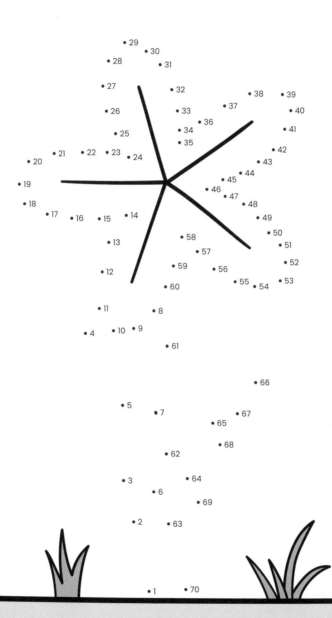

Pond

☑ Found it!

Ponds are wonderful for encouraging wildlife. They attract all sorts of insects, including dragonflies and damselflies, which lay their eggs in water, as well as newts, snails, frogs and toads. Birds and bats might come to drink from them.

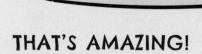

No pond?

Why don't you make one out of an old bowl?

THAT'S AMAZING!

Pond plants provide food and shelter for the animals that live in and around the pond, and, like all plants, they make the gas oxygen, which all animals need. Some pond plants, like water lilies, have their roots buried in the soil at the bottom of the pond while their leaves float on the surface.

Matching pairs

Circle the 2 frogs that are the same.

Chair

 Found it!

Chairs are designed to be comfortable to sit on. A deck chair is the perfect place to relax in the garden. These chairs fold up so that they can be stored easily when they're not being used.

THAT'S AMAZING!

The most expensive chair in the world is the 'Dragon Chair', which was sold for US $27 million.

Copy the patterns

Copy the patterns onto the chairs.

Barbecue

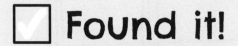 **Found it!**

A barbecue is a type of grill that's usually used to cook food outside in the open air.

THAT'S AMAZING!

Just about anything can be cooked on a barbecue, but the most popular barbecue foods are all meat-based: beef burgers, steaks and hot dogs.

Telling the time

The sausages are ready to eat! What time is it?

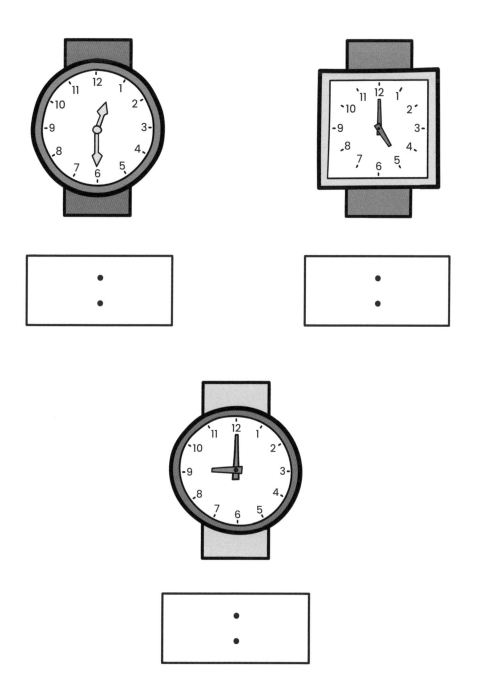

Washing line

☑ Found it!

Clean clothes, towels and sheets are hung on a washing line. They blow in the breeze to dry.

THAT'S AMAZING!

Hanging clothes on a washing line is much better for planet Earth than putting them into a powered dryer, which uses electricity.

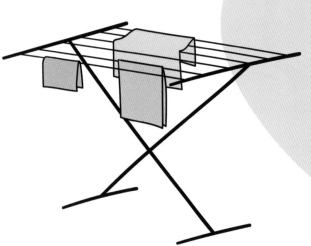

Wordsearch

Look for the 10 words hidden in the wordsearch puzzle. The hidden words will run down and across. There are no words that run backwards or on a diagonal.

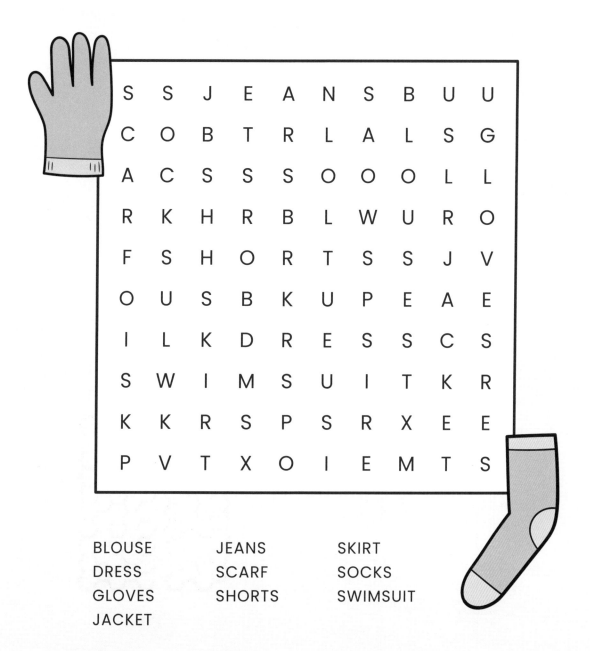

S	S	J	E	A	N	S	B	U	U
C	O	B	T	R	L	A	L	S	G
A	C	S	S	S	O	O	O	L	L
R	K	H	R	B	L	W	U	R	O
F	S	H	O	R	T	S	S	J	V
O	U	S	B	K	U	P	E	A	E
I	L	K	D	R	E	S	S	C	S
S	W	I	M	S	U	I	T	K	R
K	K	R	S	P	S	R	X	E	E
P	V	T	X	O	I	E	M	T	S

BLOUSE   JEANS   SKIRT
DRESS   SCARF   SOCKS
GLOVES   SHORTS   SWIMSUIT
JACKET

Solutions

Page 07

Page 09

Page 11

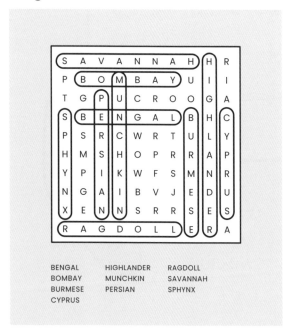

BENGAL HIGHLANDER RAGDOLL
BOMBAY MUNCHKIN SAVANNAH
BURMESE PERSIAN SPHYNX
CYPRUS

Page 13

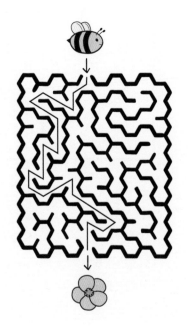

Solutions

Page 15

Page 17

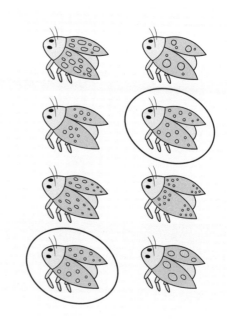

Page 19

Page 21

8	−	6	=	2
Grass		Mud		Total

0 1 2 3 4 5 6 7 8 9 10 11 12 13 14 15 16 17 18 19 20

Solutions

Page 23

Page 27

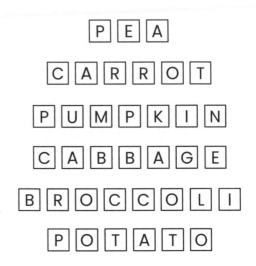

Page 31

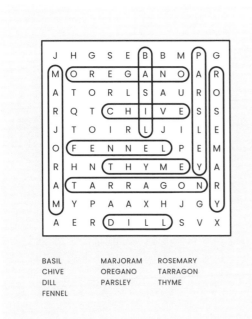

Page 35

Solutions

Page 39

Page 41

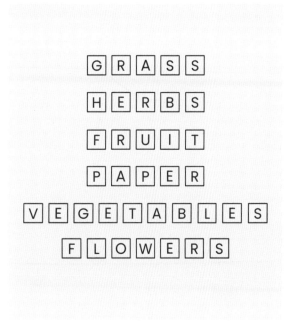

Page 43

Page 45

Solutions

Page 47

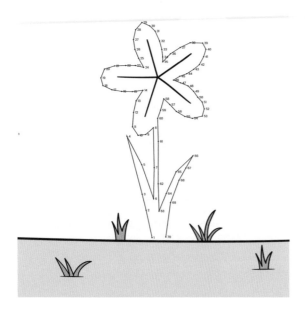

Page 49

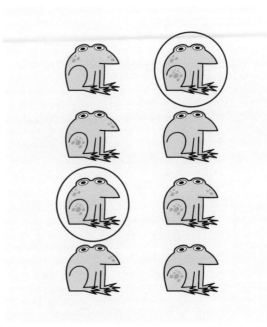

Page 53

Page 55

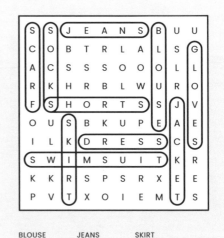

BLOUSE   JEANS   SKIRT
DRESS   SCARF   SOCKS
GLOVES   SHORTS   SWIMSUIT
JACKET

Notes on my finds

_____

_____

_____

_____

_____

_____

_____

_____

_____

_____

_____

_____

_____

_____

Notes on my finds

_____

_____

_____

_____

_____

_____

_____

_____

_____

_____

_____

_____

_____

_____

Chart of my finds

Finds by:

....

Use this chart as an index to quickly locate your finds within the book, or you can cut it out of the book and use it to find things on your travels. An adult can also use this page to confirm your finds!

Ant	☐	p.18		Grass	☐	p.34
Barbecue	☐	p.52		Herb plant	☐	p.30
Bee	☐	p.12		Pond	☐	p.48
Beetle	☐	p.16		Recycling bin	☐	p.44
Bird	☐	p.06		Snail	☐	p.22
Bird feeder	☐	p.08		Soil	☐	p.40
Cat	☐	p.10		Spider	☐	p.14
Chair	☐	p.50		Vegetable plant	☐	p.26
Flower pot	☐	p.24		Washing line	☐	p.54
Flower, purple	☐	p.32		Watering can	☐	p.46
Flower, red/pink	☐	p.28		Weed	☐	p.38
Flower, yellow	☐	p.36		Worm	☐	p.20
Fork	☐	p.42				

Find it!

Certificate

This certificate is awarded to:

....

For completing:

Find it! In the backyard

....

Date: ....